Salvador Dalí

HIS LIFE'S WORK

dosde

01

Contents. Salvador Dalí

**The Royal
Heart.** 1953

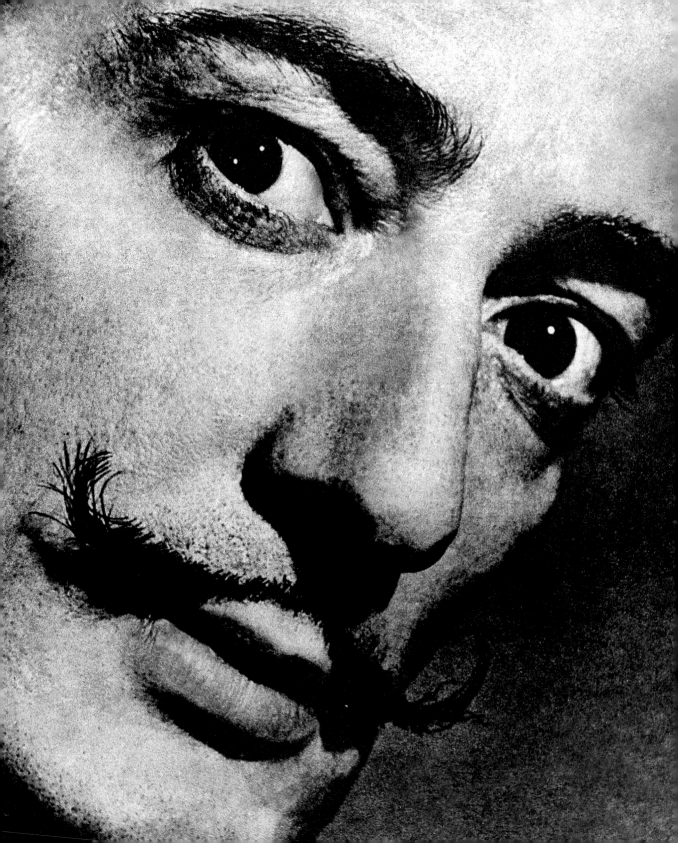

CHAPTER - 1

1904 - 1989
The total artist

Considered one of the most versatile artists of the twentieth century, Salvador Dalí i Domènech was a man driven by an insatiable curiosity. Throughout his life, the artist became interested in disciplines as varied as psychoanalysis, physics, cinema, fashion and religion, which enabled him to expand his creative resources. Because of this restless nature, the painter –born in the bosom of a wealthy family of Figueres, in northern Catalonia– experimented in his youth with Impressionism, Cubism and Neoclassicism and eventually evolved towards Surrealism, developing a style based on the use of oneiric images and the exploration of the subconscious. At the peak of popularity, Dalí alternated his artistic activity with the consolidation of his own legend, using the power of the television and the press and carrying out a pioneering approach to mass culture that did not stop him however from exploring the ultimate limits of art until the end of his active life.

A world-famous visionary genius

The road to success

Salvador Dalí from his student days exhibited a strong artistic personality. His deep knowledge of tradition and alternative cultural trends led the painter to repeatedly rebel against an academic system that he considered obsolete, to the point that he even came to be expelled from the *Escuela de Bellas Artes* (the School of Fine Arts) for undermining his teachers. At the same time, the innate ability of the artist to draw from and appropriate the most diverse of styles quickly positioned him as one of the great promises of his generation. After a period of experimentation in the context of the Spanish avant-garde scene, Dalí finally showed off all his potential when he joined forces with the Surrealist movement, which helped him achieve international recognition.

Magnetic presence

Aware of the changing role of the artist in the consumer society, Dalí took care of every detail of his public image, ranging from his original moustache to his form of expression. This way, he rapidly became the centre of attention.

1919
IS THE YEAR
in which Dalí exhibited his paintings in public for the first time, in the framework of a collective exhibition held in Figueres.

Dalí and Lorca

During the decade of the twenties, the Catalan painter (pictured, on the right) and the Granada poet (in the centre) established a fruitful dialogue through joint projects and the exchange of ideas.

25
YEARS OF AGE
was how old Dalí was when he met Gala. The meeting with his future wife implied both a turning point in the painter's life as well as in his work.

✳ **A multifaceted artist**
Dalí's talents ranged from oil painting to jewellery design, lithography and theatre set creation.

✳ **True to his land**
The painter incorporated the landscape of the Catalan region of Empordà in his works, where he spent many years.

1927
IS THE YEAR
that Salvador Dalí started to introduce surrealist elements into many of his paintings.

1904
Born on May the 11th in Figueres, where he starts painting.

1922
He moves to Madrid. Becomes friends with Federico García Lorca and Luis Buñuel.

1929
He is in contact with the Surrealists in Paris. He meets Gala.

1934
He travels to New York for the first time.

1940
His exile begins in the United States.

1942
He publishes his autobiography, *The secret life of Salvador Dalí.*

1948
He returns to Spain and develops Nuclear-Mysticism.

1958
He and Gala married in a church ceremony.

1974
Dalí Theatre-Museum of Figueres opens.

1982
Gala dies. Dalí obtains the title of Marquis.

1989
He dies in Figueres on the 23rd of January.

Dalí and his sister Ana María, in Cadaqués, in 1925

Dalí and Gala arriving at New York, in 1936

A life made art
Throughout his career, Salvador Dalí used painting in order to reflect the events that happened during his life, so that his works gained in depth and acquired multiple interpretations. The Catalan artist developed a wide range of symbolic images, often indecipherable, to refer to his family and his childhood traumas, which became an inexhaustible source of inspiration. Dalí's wife, Gala, was another key part of the creative universe of a painter specialised in exploring the innermost recesses of the human being.

Del Monte Lodge, 1947
Dalí, accompanied by Gala, created a painting in the period in which he was also writing the book *50 Secrets of Magic Craftsmanship*.

Dalí and Walt Disney
The Spanish painter worked for the American filmmaker on a failed project. Harpo Marx and Alfred Hitchcock also called on his services.

Paris, 1977
Dalí, in the Hotel Meurice, with two models and the work *Retrospective Bust of a Woman*, one of the most well-known of his surrealist objects.

Staging of Surrealism

Taking advantage of the mass media's capacity to reach out to the public, Dalí rapidly learned how to project an image of a provocative and an eccentric artist which set him apart from the rest of his contemporaries. The painter did not hesitate to transfer his pictorial ideas to real surroundings, and converted each of his appearances into a creative act intended to attract public attention. Through the integration of surrealist language into everyday life, the artist not only anticipated the phenomenon of the *performances*, but also helped blur the boundaries between academic tradition and popular culture.

84
YEARS OF AGE
was Salvador Dalí when he died. The painter was buried in the Theatre-Museum of Figueres.

1929
IS THE YEAR
in which *Un Chien Andalou* premiered in Paris, the painter's debut as a cinema screenwriter.

Mediatic figure
Dalí regularly appeared on television, especially in the United States. One of his most impressive appearances came in the year 1961 on the programme *The Ed Sullivan* show, where he showed his gun painting method.

The artist, painting *The Battle of Tetuán*, in 1962

Dalí, in 1975, with one of his stereoscopic works

The culmination of his career

In the seventies, when Salvador Dalí was in the final stages of his professional life, the artist was totally dedicated to the creation of the Dalí Theatre-Museum of Figueres. Inaugurated in the year 1974, the centre became a representation of the singular inner world of the artist, both for its design as for its collection, ranging from the pictorial incursions of his adolescence to the experiments that he carried out in his final years.

Galatea Tower. Exterior of Dalí Theatre-Museum

Theatre-Museum courtyard

Poet Federico García Lorca and Dalí, in Figueres, in 1927

CHAPTER - 2

1920 - 1928
The student years

Gifted with an innate talent, Salvador Dalí showed a keen interest in drawing and painting from a very early age. Thanks to the unconditional support of his mother and father, who were quick to grasp the enormous potential of their son, the boy was able to practice continuously both in school as well as in his free time and, thus, rapidly refined and improved his technique. Likewise, from childhood the painter was exposed to all types of cultural trends that developed outside the official canons, such as the post-impressionist movements, a fact that helped him obtain a much broader and uninhibited vision of the artistic medium. With this sound foundation of knowledge and growing experience, the young Dalí was amply prepared to embark on a promising academic career in the city of Madrid, where, besides being able to work on and perfect his range of skills, he also had the opportunity to integrate into the more vanguardist intellectual circles of Spain.

LEFT
The Smiling Venus
1921
Oil on cardboard
51.5 × 50.3 cm

RIGHT
Portrait of my Father
1920
Oil on canvas
91 × 66.5 cm

The painter's beginnings

The first artistic style with which Dalí felt fully identified was Impressionism, which he discovered at twelve years of age through the work of Ramon Pichot, a family acquaintance who had formed part of the Catalan modernist scene. Fascinated by the work of Pichot, the painter spent much of his youth exploring the visual possibilities of the impressionist technique. Using long strokes and a palette of vibrant and bright colours, the young Dalí depicted on canvas his favourite landscapes from the north coast of Catalonia, such as the Bay of Cadaqués and Cap de Creus, a setting of great visual force distinguished by its rocky profiles shaped by the wind and sea. The family environment was also a constant source of inspiration for the future surrealist genius, who in works such as *Portrait of my Father* was already able to capture the essence of human psychology.

By 1920, as his school years were nearing an end, Dalí enriched his language with elements typical of Pointillism, Expressionism and Fauvism, more advanced styles that provided his work with greater freshness. The artist alternated his more innovative side with the study of the legacy of the classical masters of painting. Amongst his favourite artists were Velázquez, Goya, El Greco, Dürer and, above all, Raphael, to whom he wished to pay tribute by painting *Self-Portrait with Raphaelesque Neck*, showing great self-confidence by comparing himself to the Renaissance icon.

The student residence

Following his father's orders, in 1922 Dalí moved to Madrid to begin his studies of Fine Arts at the *Royal Academy of San Fernando*, the most prestigious institution of the country, where all the painters went who wanted to guarantee stable future employment. The young man, who was only eighteen, decided to settle in the *Residencia de Estudiantes*, a centre of progressive character intended to supplement the intellectual formation of its guests through interdisciplinary cultural exchange and the dissemination of new ideas generated in the rest of Europe. Within this dynamic environment, ideal for intellectual development, Dalí became friends with other young people like himself, including the writer Pepín Bello, filmmaker Luis Buñuel and poet Federico García Lorca, which would mark his personal evolution. Marked by sexual tension and contrasting personalities, the

BELOW
Self-Portrait with Raphaelesque Neck
1921
Oil on canvas
40.5 × 53 cm

LEFT
Figure at a Window
1925
Oil
105 × 74.5 cm

RIGHT
**Self-Portrait with
L'Humanité**
1923
Tempera, oil and collage
on cardboard
105 × 75 cm

NEXT PAGE, ABOVE LEFT
Figure on the Rocks
1926
Oil on wood
27 × 41 cm

relationship with Lorca was particularly intense, and led to the development of common themes such as love, frustration and putrefaction.

During his years at the *Royal Academy of San Fernando* Dalí experimented with diverse trends simultaneously incorporating resources from Cubism, Futurism and Metaphysical painting into his works. Aiming to equip himself with his own identity, the artist also turned to tradition, emulating the accuracy and attention to detail characteristic of neoclassical painter Dominique Ingres in order to create compositions of an almost photographic realism, including *Figure at a Window,* where the Catalan painter portrayed his sister Ana María as she watched the coast of Cadaqués.

Thanks to his technical mastery and in-depth knowledge of the latest trends, Dalí quickly won the admiration of his peers. The artist's popularity steadily grew from 1925, when he had the opportunity to show off his talent in public events of great impact such as the *Exhibition of the Iberian Artists Society* in Madrid and his first solo exhibition at the Dalmau Galleries in Barcelona, which consolidated him as one of the most interesting artists of his generation.

PREVIOUS PAGE, ABOVE RIGHT
Portrait of Luis Buñuel
1924
Oil on canvas
70 × 60 cm

PREVIOUS PAGE, BELOW
Girl from Figueres
1926
Oil on wood
20.8 × 21.5 cm

The pre-surrealist phase

In April 1926, accompanied by his aunt and his sister, Dalí first visited Paris. During his stay in the French capital, the painter met Picasso, to whom he showed his work and he immersed himself in the busy life of Parisian cafés, converted into meeting points for the Spanish colony that wanted to break into the cultural scene of the city. Moreover, Dalí was able to visit the Louvre, where he spent hours contemplating the works of Leonardo, Raphael and Ingres.

The trip to Paris made a deep impression on Dalí, who probably returned to Madrid convinced that his future was going to be established in the French capital. This plan made him move definitively away from the *Royal Academy of San Fernando*, whose conservatism clashed with the artist's desire for cre-

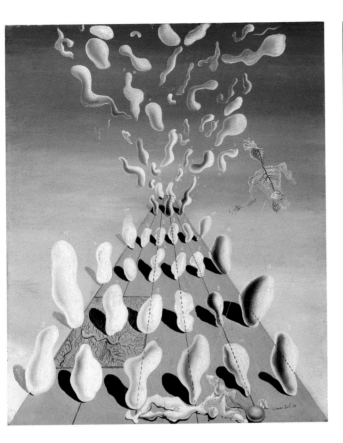

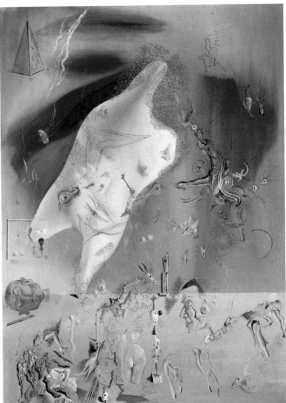

ative freedom. Thus, Dalí decided to challenge the institution by refusing to be examined by a court which, according to him, was not qualified to evaluate him. Immediately expelled, the artist returned to his native Figueres, where he dedicated his time to searching for new ways of expression.

From 1927, Dalí approached the tenets of Surrealism, an artistic and literary movement heir of Dadaism that advocated the validity of the dream world and irrational impulses. The artist was already familiar with the workings of the unconscious in the *Residencia de Estudiantes*, where he could access the work of Sigmund Freud, and was inspired by the paintings of Yves Tanguy and Joan Miró to redefine his style. Although still reluctant to be classed as a Surrealist, Dalí adopted many of the features characteristic of this movement in the pictures carried out during this period, recreating oneiric-like spaces populated by strange figures without any apparent connection. In paintings such as *Honey is Sweeter than Blood*, the strong personality of the artist was reflected in the use of a particularly aggressive iconography. The division of the canvases into two half-planes delimited by a line was also another constant of the production of the pre-surrealist phase, which laid the foundations of the most revolutionary and imaginative works of the Catalan painter.

PREVIOUS PAGE
Study for Honey is Sweeter than Blood
1926
Oil on wood
37.8 × 46.2 cm

LEFT
Inaugural Gooseflesh
1928
Oil on cardboard
76 × 63.2 cm

RIGHT
Little Ashes
1927-1928
Oil on wood
64 × 48 cm

CHAPTER - 3

1929 - 1935
The emergence of Surrealism

After the First World War, Surrealism converted into one of the most influential avant-garde movements thanks to its revolutionary approach, which sought to transform human existence in order to create a better world. However, in the late twenties the movement reached a critical point. The communist sympathies of the leader of the group, the French poet and writer André Breton, caused the disaffection or opposition of those intellectuals who wanted to confine their actions to solely the artistic field. Furthermore, the authors' capacity of subversion seemed to be exhausted owing to the repeated use of the same creative formulas. In this context, the emergence of Salvador Dalí was essential in order to ensure the continuity of the movement. Possessor of an imagination and technical skill far superior to that of the majority of his peers, the Catalan painter took Surrealism to another level, with far-reaching contributions both in theory and iconography.

**The Enigma of Desire
or Ma mère, ma mère,
ma mère**
1929
Oil on canvas
110.5 × 150.5 cm

Portrait of Paul Éluard
1929
Oil on cardboard
33 × 25 cm

Significant relationships

In April 1929 Salvador Dalí returned to Paris to work with his friend Luis Buñuel on the development of the short film known as *Un Chien Andalou* (An Andalusian Dog). Released in June of that same year, the film was formed by a series of oneiric images with a strong visual impact, such as those scenes that make up the opening sequence, in which the filmmaker severs an eye with a razor blade. With the desire to break into the art market of the French capital, Dalí also made the most of his stay in order to make new contacts. Thus, through the mediation of the Catalan painter Joan Miró, his main supporter, the artist was able to make the acquaintance of Belgian art dealer Camille Goemans, who, besides offering him a contract to sell his work exclusively, introduced him to the painter René Magritte and surrealist poet Paul Eluard, whose ideas enthralled Dalí.

After spending two months in Paris, Dalí moved to Cadaqués to plunge into a particularly fertile creative period. Added to the repeated readings of the

LEFT
The Invisible Man
1929-1932
Oil on canvas
140 × 81 cm

RIGHT
The Lugubrious Game
1929
Oil and collage
on cardboard
44.4 × 30.3 cm

NEXT PAGE
**Close-ups of
The Lugubrious Game**

writings of André Breton, the recent meetings he had had with various French intellectuals accelerated his evolution into a style that was fully based on surrealist postulates. Incorporating the theories of Sigmund Freud in the *Interpretation of Dreams*, the Catalan artist began to work on various hallucinatory scenes that, despite their apparent irrationality, were the result of painstaking and time-consuming work, based on the systematisation of ideas and much more intimate images.

The Lugubrious Game –which is also known as *The Mournful Game*– was the picture that opened the new pictorial period of Dalí. On canvas, the artist recorded his major phobias and obsessions, which were related to sex, shame and conflict with the father figure. To do this, Dalí used symbolic images such as a sleeping head, grasshoppers, ants, lions and stones, which appeared repeatedly in posterior works, thereby strengthening the internal coherence of the painter's surrealist production.

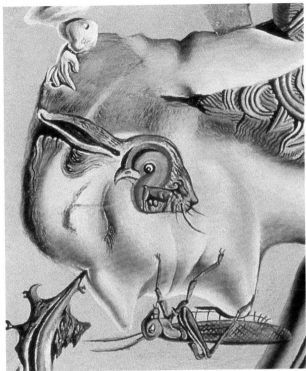

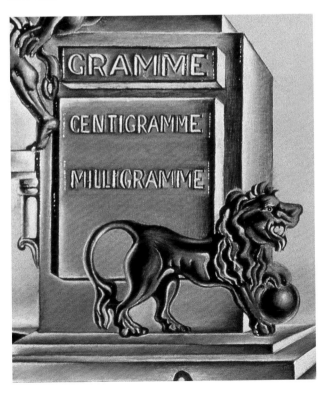

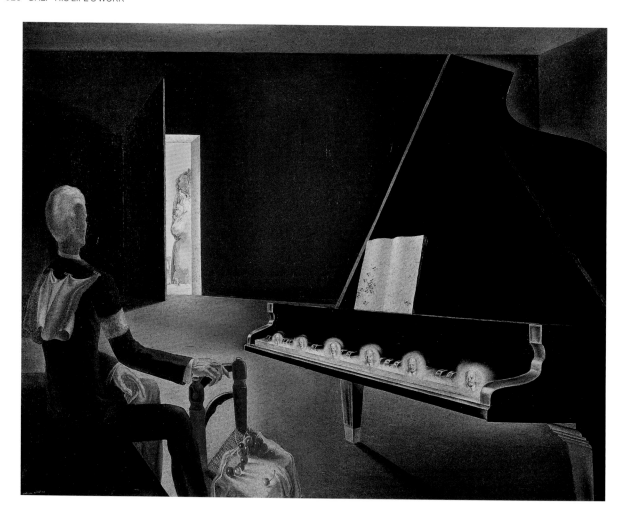

The arrival of Gala

In the summer of 1929 in Cadaqués Dalí received the visit of the Goemans, who were accompanied by Buñuel, Magritte and his wife and Paul Éluard and his spouse, Gala. Born in 1894 in Kazán (Russia) with the name Elena Ivanovna Diakonova, the wife of the French poet stood out for her seductive character, which had led her to become the muse of the main promoters of Surrealism. Overcome by mutual fascination, Dalí and Gala began a romantic relationship that was even approved of by Eluard. Under the influence of his new partner, who helped him to break free mentally, the artist addressed *The Great Masturbator*. Presided over by the self-portrait of the painter –inspired by a rock in Cape Creus– the canvas referred to ongoing tensions between sexual desire and the satisfaction of pleasure, while alluding to the flight from the family nest, which was strongly opposed to Dalí's relationship with Gala.

PREVIOUS PAGE, ABOVE
Hallucination: Six Apparitions of Lenin on a Grand Piano
1931. Oil on canvas
114 × 146 cm

PREVIOUS PAGE, BELOW LEFT
Egg on the plate (without the plate)
1932. Oil on canvas
60 × 41.9 cm

FORMER PAGE, BELOW RIGHT
The Old Age of William Tell
1931
Oil on canvas
98 × 140 cm

The Great Masturbator. 1929. Oil on canvas. 110 × 150 cm

Surrealist objects

Irrational constructions

From 1931 Salvador Dalí alternated painting with the creation of surrealist objects, a practice that had its precedent in the Dadaist constructions of French artist Marcel Duchamp and which was promoted by André Breton in order to transfer the ideas of the unconscious to the material world. Formed by seemingly random combinations of different everyday objects, these pieces of striking design intended to overcome the traditional concept of sculpture, since in their elaboration rational criteria was ignored. Although the surrealist objects had no practical uses, Dalí nonetheless tried to sell some of his creations. However, difficulties encountered in the manufacturing processes meant that the artist's plans couldn't be brought to fruition.

❶ Retrospective Bust of Woman
1933
Dalí adorned this female sculpture with some of his most representative symbols, like figures from Millet's *The Angelus*, bread and ants.

London, 1936. Dalí, dressed as a diver, alongside Paul Éluard, Nush and Herbert Read in the *International Exposition of Surrealism* held in the British capital.

❶

❷

Venus de Milo with Drawers
1936/1964
Of painted bronze, it symbolises the deepest psychological mysteries of sexual desire.

❸

Shoe and Glass of Milk. Surrealist object of symbolic function
1931/1973
Hanging over the drinking glass is a sugar cube decorated with a shoe.

10
MODELS
of the *Lobster-Telephone* were manufactured by Salvador Dalí. Four of these copies are the colour red, while the other six are white.

❹

Lobster-Telephone
1936
Dalí designed this object to be included as part of the decoration of the home of art collector Edward James.

❺

The Mae West Lips Sofa
1936-1937
It was designed for the work *Face of Mae West's Face which may be used as a Surrealist Apartment*, a setting in which a chimney was the nose of the actress and two pictures were her eyes.

Aphrodisiac Dinner Jacket. The glasses on the jacket contained mint liquor.

Rainy Taxi. The inside of the autombile is equipped with an irrigation system.

Dalí Mannequin Chair. Sculpture-like, it is in the Theatre-Museum Dalí.

**The Persistence of
Memory**
1931
Oil on canvas
24.1 × 33 cm

From Paris to Portlligat

When Dalí returned to Paris in the autumn of 1929, his name was becoming well-known in avant-garde circles. *Un Chien Andalou* (An Andalusian Dog)was being projected on the commercial cinema circuit with a good reception from the public, while the Goemans Gallery was in the midst of preparations to hold the artist's first solo exhibition in the French capital. The exhibition, whose catalogue was prefaced by André Breton, focused on the most recent works, including *The First Days of Spring*, in which Dalí combined memories of childhood with the preoccupations of his adult life. Despite its limited impact on the Parisian press, the exhibition turned out to be a bestseller, at the same time bringing the artist closer to Surrealism. The artist's definitive entrance into the movement led by Breton came at the end of the year, coinciding with the publication of the last edition of the magazine *The Surrealist Revolution*, which included the full script of *Un Chien Andalou* and reproductions of two of Dalí's paintings.

While the entry of Dalí in the Surrealist Movement was made official, the artist's relationship with his family was at its worst. The tension that had begun with the arrival of Gala increased upon learning that the painter had exhibited in Paris a drawing of the Sacred Heart with the inscription "Sometimes, with pleasure I spit on the portrait of my mother". Dalí's father demanded an apology from his son, but the latter refused and eventually was expelled from the family home and disinherited. Incapable of moving away from his homeland, in 1930 the painter bought a shack in Portlligat, a small fishing village located in a cove of Cape Creus. Object of several extensions, the house was the only stable residence of Dalí, who found an inexhaustible source of inspiration in his impressive surroundings.

The stunning landscape of Portlligat was precisely the scenario for *The Persistence of Memory*, a work in which Dalí expressed the anguish of human beings to control time by the means of three melted clocks that, according to the painter, were based on Camembert cheese. First exhibited in 1931 at the Pierre Colle Art Gallery, the painting fascinated the public and raised all kinds of interpretations, such as those that related the clocks to the *Theory of Relativity* of Albert Einstein.

ABOVE LEFT
The Weaning of Furniture-Nutrition
1934
Oil on wood
17.78 × 24.13 cm

BELOW LEFT
The First Days of Spring
1929
Oil and collage on wood
49.5 × 64 cm

RIGHT
Enigmatic Elements in a Landscape
1934
Oil on wood
72.8 × 59.5 cm

ABOVE LEFT
Catalan Bread
1932
Oil on canvas
24 × 33 cm

BELOW LEFT
**Atmospheric Skull
Sodomizing a Grand
Piano**
1934
Oil on wood
14 × 17.8 cm

RIGHT
**The Ghost of Vermeer
of Delft Which Can Be
Used as a Table**
Around 1934
Oil on wood
18.1 × 13.97 cm

The Paranoiac-Critical method

Despite his identification with the Surrealist group, during the first half of the thirties Salvador Dalí differed from the rest of his colleagues of the time by developing a system of his own creation that he named the *Paranoiac-Critical Method*. With this unique technique, inspired partly by psychoanalytic studies conducted by Jacques Lacan at the same time, the painter defended the interpretation of reality according to ones own particular obsessions. One of the keys to the procedure devised by Dalí consisted of the development of double or multiple images, which were capable of freeing the viewer's imagination and giving rise to different interpretations. The optical distortion of figures was another tool that was used by the painter to implement his method, as was reflected in paintings such as *Atmospheric Skull Sodomizing a Grand Piano*, in which the artist gave a skull an elastic appearance in order to express his fear of death and venereal diseases.

Dalí's new artistic approach was praised by Breton, knowing that it could be successfully applied in painting as well as in poetry and filmmaking. By requiring the author to play an active role and by asserting the validity of figurative art to represent the irrational world, the creative system designed by the Catalan artist renewed the methodology used traditionally by the followers of Surrealism, who until then had made use of the *automatic drawing* technique in order to express the ideas of the unconscious in a passive way.

Personal mythology

The utilisation of the Paranoiac-Critical method led to the emergence of several recurring images in Salvador Dalí's work, such as food products. Bread, considered to be man's staple food and a symbol of life intrinsically linked to religious tradition, served as a metaphor for sexual desire by taking on phallic forms, while the incorporation of fried eggs has been interpreted as an allusion to fertilization or returning to the womb. For their part, the chops were a representation of eroticism and the fantasy of devouring a loved one.

BELOW
Portrait of Gala with Two Lamb Chops in Equilibrium upon Her Shoulder
Around 1934
Oil on wood
6.8 × 8.8 cm

LEFT
**The Architectonic
Angelus of Millet**
1933
Oil on canvas
73 × 60 cm

ABOVE RIGHT
**Archaeological
Reminiscence of
Millet's Angelus**
Around 1934
Oil on wood
31.75 × 39.4 cm

Between the years 1933 and 1934, much of the production of Dalí revolved around the picture named *The Angelus,* a popular painting carried out by French artist Jean-Francois Millet and produced in the second half of the nineteenth century. The Catalan artist confessed that this work took him back to his childhood, when he had seen a reproduction of it for the first time, and that it also reflected his deepest fears. According to Dalí, the country scene recreated by Millet, protagonised by a peasant couple who interrupt their work in order to pray, contained hidden references to oedipal anxiety and castration, and could be interpreted as a variant of the myth of Saturn, in which parents devour their own children. From this analysis, detailed in a long essay written in 1933 in which was also mentioned the Paranoiac-Critical method, the artist integrated in his pictorial universe the most recognisable elements of the original picture, giving them new meanings. Thus, in works such as *The Architectonic Angelus of Millet* two peasants were represented as giant soft sensual shapes and white lines, with the coast of Cadaqués used as a backdrop to the painting.

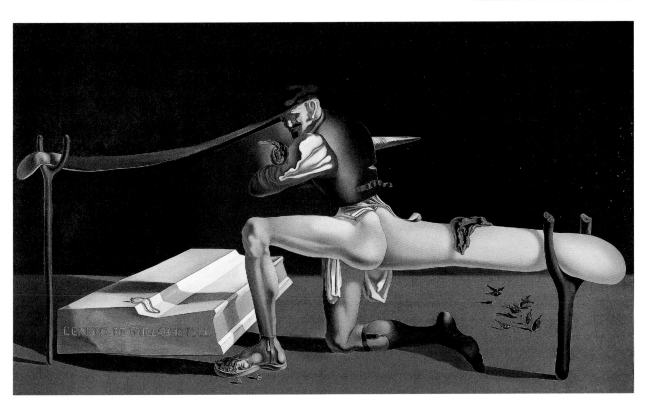

Tensions with Breton

In the month of February 1934, after a civil marriage with Gala, Dalí participated in the *Salon des Independents*, one of the most important events of the Parisian art scene or art calender, distinguished for publicising alternative trends to academic conventions. With this initiative, the painter completely distanced himself from other Surrealists, who had agreed to stay on the margin of the exposition in order to be consistent with their subversive speech. The affront was even greater when it emerged that one of the works chosen for the event was *The Enigma of William Tell*, in which a disproportionate figure displayed the face of the leader of the Russian Revolution, Vladimir Lenin, political icon of Surrealism.

Disgusted with this provocation, Breton tried to destroy the painting, who then decided to convene an urgent meeting of the surrealist group to decide the expulsion of Dalí, whom was accused of moving away from the communist doctrine and of making excessive concessions to please his potential patrons. The Catalan artist attended the meeting wearing several wool sweaters with a thermometer in his mouth, turning the trial into a hilarious show. After defining himself as a true Surrealist and arguing that his vision of Lenin could not be subject to any censorship because it came from the unconscious, Dalí obtained the acquittal of his companions, who were unable to stop from laughing at the farce designed by the painter. Once tensions were resolved with Breton, Dalí again directed his energies to the promotion of his work, emphasizing his intellectual independence.

PREVIOUS PAGE, BELOW RIGHT
Geological Destiny
1933
Oil on wood
21 × 16 cm

ABOVE
The Enigma of William Tell
Around 1933
Oil on canvas
201.3 × 346.5 cm

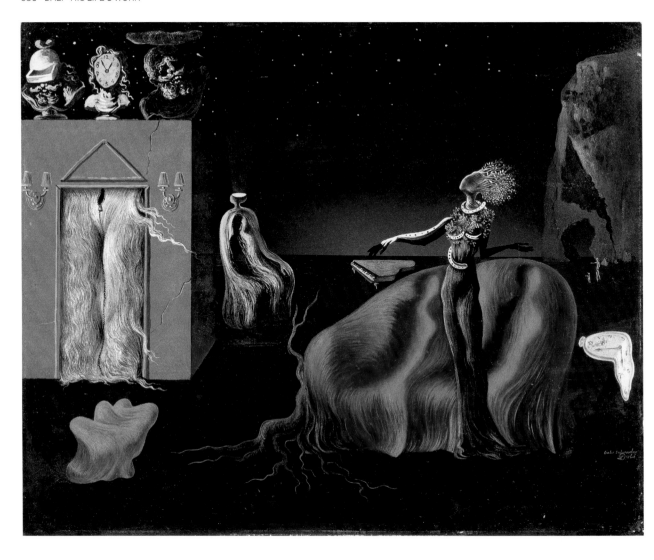

ABOVE
Singularities
Around 1935
Oil and collage
on board
40.5 × 50 cm

The United States trip

Three weeks after his first solo exhibition was inaugurated in London, on the 14th of November 1934 Dalí landed in the city of New York with his inseparable companion Gala. Before his arrival, the North American public had already become familiar with his work thanks to the tireless advocacy of art dealer Julien Levy, whose relationship with the surrealist genius went back to the year 1931, when he had acquired the picture *The Persistence of Memory*. Levy had invited Dalí to attend an exhibition in his own gallery which sought to provide a broad overview of the artist's work by means of more than twenty paintings. The appointment was a bestseller and was widely covered by the New York media, who devoted countless interviews to him and gave him rave reviews.

Aware of the commercial possibilities that were on offer in the United States, a country receptive to new ideas, Dalí enhanced his most extravagant side in order to catch the attention of the public. Moreover, the painter strengthened his position within Surrealism by lecturing in prestigious centres such as the Museum of Modern Art of New York, an institution that ended up being fundamental to the dissemination of Dalí's work. The trip came to a close with a farewell party at the *Coq Rouge Restaurant*. The guests at the event had to go dressed up as their favourite dream, which set a precedent for future artistic *performances*. Dalí came with a bandaged head and a glass case on his chest containing a bra in honour of the organiser of the event, Caresse Crosby, the inventor of this feminine top. Gala, meanwhile, wore a skirt comprised of red cellophane and a hat decorated with the figure of a baby and a lobster. Her outfit caused a huge scandal, since many people thought the baby was referring to the murder of the son of aviator Charles Lindbergh, an event that had shocked North Americans. Despite the controversy, Dalí returned to France with the certainty that he would soon succeed in America.

LEFT
**The Spectre of
Sex-appeal**
Around 1934
Oil on wood
18 × 14 cm

RIGHT
**The Face of Mae West
which may be used as a
Surrealistic Apartment**
1934-1935
Gouache on
newspaper paper
31 × 17 cm

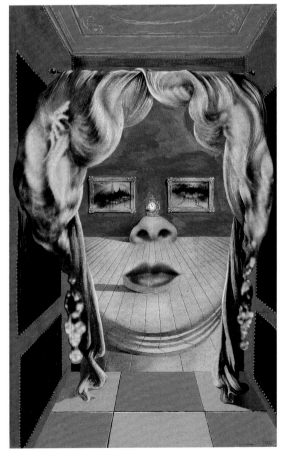

CHAPTER - 4

1936 - 1940
The war and the subconscious

In the late 1930's Europe stepped into a turbulent period with tragic consequences. In Spain, the rise of a faction of the army against the Republican government led to a bloody civil war that ended with the establishment of a fascist regime led by General Francisco Franco. Meanwhile, in Germany, Adolf Hitler was managing to carry out his expansionist plans by means of an aggressive foreign policy that ended up triggering off the beginning of World War II. Forced to leave his homeland after the onset of hostilities, Salvador Dalí found in this threatening environment a new source of inspiration for his work. With full stylistic maturity, the painter managed to successfully convey the anguish associated with the war in order to create compositions that were as disturbing as they were suggestive, while at the same time he continued to experiment with the artistic possibilities of his Paranoiac-Critical method, enriching an increasingly popular symbolic universe.

Between horror and fame

When the Spanish Civil War commenced, in July 1936, Dalí was in London, where he had gone to inaugurate a solo show at the influential art gallery *Alex Reid & Lefevre* and participate in the *International Surrealist Exhibition*, a major event for the Surrealist movement to take root in Britain. While waiting to see how world events would take shape, the painter chose to move to Paris. It was there he received the news of the death of Lorca, who was executed in Granada by the Fascists. The murder of whom had been one of his closest friends was a hard blow to the Catalan artist, who decided to take refuge in his work and maintain apparent political neutrality.

After a stay in Italy, in December Dalí visited the United States for the second time. Received as a star by the press, as evidenced by his appearance on the cover of *Time* magazine, the artist established his first contacts with the film industry in Hollywood, and even began working with Harpo Marx on the script of a film that never got to be made. He also exhibited some of his latest works at the *Julien Levy Gallery*, including *Soft Construction with Boiled Beans*, which included references to the dramatic Spanish situation.

Inevitably, references to the civil war reappeared in later compositions such as the allegorical painting *Spain*, in which Dalí drew a female figure from a war scene of Leonardo da Vinci.

The secrets of the subconscious

While civil war raged on, the trajectory of Dalí was at a peak. The painter could count on the financial backing of Edward James, a British patron who provided him with regular income in exchange for managing his work, so that he would not have to be concerned about mundane everyday matters and devote himself to consolidating his own artistic style. Thanks to his knowledge of psychoanalysis, the artist developed new symbols that fostered the enigmatic character of his paintings. Open drawers were one of the most effective contributions. Integrated into the body of female characters they served as a metaphor for the secrets that one does not even dare tell oneself, and that can only come to light through therapy. The burning giraffe became another icon characteristic of that period. According to the

BELOW
Palladio's corridor of dramatic disguise
1938
Oil on canvas
73 × 104 cm

BELOW
**Swans Reflecting
Elephants**
1937
Oil on canvas
51 × 77 cm

NEXT PAGE, ABOVE
**Metamorphosis of
Narcissus**
1937
Oil on canvas
51.1 × 78.1 cm

NEXT PAGE, BELOW
The Dream
1937
Oil on canvas
51 × 78 cm

painter, his intention was to create a representation of the "male cosmic apocalyptic monster", but the image also could be interpreted as a reference to the war and the absurdity of human existence.

In addition to renewing his iconography, Dalí continued to defend the usefulness of his Paranoiac-Critical method. In that sense, his most ambitious work was *Metamorphosis of Narcissus*, which was supplemented by a poem. Based on the Greek myth of Narcissus, the young man who ended up falling in love with his own reflection in a pond after being punished by the gods, Dalí experimented with the use of double images simultaneously addressing various concepts such as egotism, the human drama of love, sexual ambiguity, transformation in death and the influence of Gala. The importance of *Metamorphosis of Narcissus* became evident in the year 1938, when Dalí took this picture to a meeting with Sigmund Freud in London. The founding father of psychoanalysis expressed his admiration for the technical mastery achieved by the Spanish artist as well as his interest in delving into the genesis of the work. Exultant, Dalí felt that Freud's observations were an endorsement of his Paranoiac-Critical method and, by extension, the surrealist movement as a whole.

Monsters of the Civil War

Premonition of the struggle

Unlike his friends Lorca and Buñuel, during the 1930's Salvador Dalí did not commit himself politically in order to ensure the possibility of returning to Spain in the future. Despite this uncertainty, in *Soft Construction with Boiled Beans* the artist was able to express the tension experienced in Spain in the months prior to the war. Converted into a symbol of fratricidal struggle, the work is one of the most disturbing compositions created by Dali, who contrasted the brightness of the Mediterranean landscape with the ferocity of a monstrous being that was composed of different elements of a human body strangling and trampling itself in an absurd exercise in self-destruction.

➡

Soft Construction with Boiled Beans
1936
Oil on canvas
99.9 × 100 cm

6

MONTHS
was the time that passed between the completion of the painting and the start of the Civil War.

1934

IS THE YEAR
Dalí carried out the first sketches of the work. That year, several revolts showed the deterioration of Spanish politics.

Madrid, 1972. Dalí, in the Pardo Palace, showing dictator Francisco Franco the equestrian portrait of his eldest granddaughter, Carmen Martinez Bordiú.

Cannibalism as a metaphor

Shortly after the civil war commenced Dali developed *Autumnal Cannibalism*, where he relapsed into the absurdity of battle. The work shows two amorphous beings devouring each other. On the head of one of them is an apple, referring to the legend of William Tell. Thus, cannibalism is also related to the father that is willing to sacrifice his own son, such as the cruel Saturn who was portrayed by Spanish painter Francisco de Goya.

Autumnal Cannibalism. 1936. Oil on canvas. 65.1 × 65.1 cm

Saturn devouring his son. Francisco de Goya. 1820-1823. Oil on canvas. 14.6 × 83 cm

Visage of the War. 1940. Oil on wood. 64 × 79 cm

The end of a period

After another triumphant stay in the city of New York, in June 1939 Salvador Dalí was expelled from the surrealist group. The desire for notoriety and the differing opinions of the painter had exhausted the patience of Breton, who accused the artist of monotony in order to please his potential patrons. Moreover, Dalí's obsession with Adolf Hitler played a key role in his expulsion, made explicit in *The Enigma of Hitler*, a work in which he turned to the image of a broken telephone to express the lack of communication and anguish of the European countries with the advance of Nazism. The break with the Surrealists served to certify the independence of Dalí, whose popularity continued growing steadily, thanks in part to his forays into other artistic disciplines such as the fields of literature and theatre. Thus, when the Second World War broke out, the painter had sufficient resources to draw from in order to ensure his tranquility.

PREVIOUS PAGE, LEFT
The Enigma of Hitler
1939. Oil on canvas
95 × 141 cm

PREVIOUS PAGE, RIGHT
Average Pagan Landscape
1937. Oil on canvas
38.5 × 46.5 cm

ABOVE
Impressions of Africa
1938. Oil on canvas
91.5 × 117.5 cm

CHAPTER - 5

1940 - 1948
Exile in the United States

The Second World War led to the dismantlement of the European avant-garde scene. The German occupation of France and the Nazi persecution of modern art meant that many of the most influential people of the time, amongst them Salvador Dalí himself, made the decision to move to the United States. This exodus of artists and intellectuals made the epicentre of cultural innovation move from the French capital of Paris to New York, a city in which new experimental trends started to emerge. The influence that Surrealism exerted on movements such as Abstract Expressionism reevaluated the figure of Dalí, who in prewar years had already undertaken an aggressive promotional campaign to curry favor with the North-American public. Taking advantage of this pre-eminent position during his exile the Catalan painter turned to building up his legend, by starring in exhibitions in the most important of art galleries and by lending his talents to other types of media.

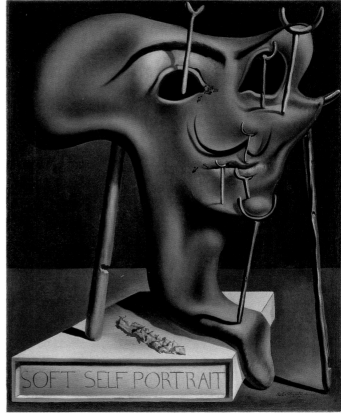

LEFT
**Poetry of America –
The Cosmic Athletes**
1943
Oil on canvas
116.8 × 78.7 cm

RIGHT
**Soft Self-Portrait with
Fried Bacon**
1941
Oil on canvas
61.3 × 50.8 cm

NEXT PAGE
**Slave Market with
the Disappearing
Bust of Voltaire**
1940
Oil on canvas
46.5 × 65.5 cm

The consolidation of the myth

In August 1940, two months after German troops paraded through the centre of Paris, Salvador Dalí and Gala departed from Lisbon to United States, where they would stay for the next eight years. The couple moved into the mansion of his friend and patron Caresse Crosby, located in the state of Virginia. There the painter worked intensively on his autobiography, *The Secret Life of Salvador Dalí*, in which he dispensed with documentary rigour to compose an extraordinary account of his career, intended to praise his achievements. Moreover, the artist made many pictures for his next exhibition in the gallery of art dealer Julien Levy, including *Soft Self-Portrait with Fried Bacon*. Inspired by the breakfasts of the Saint Regis Hotel in New York, the oil painting shows the amorphous face of the painter supported by various crutches.

Held between April and May 1941, the exhibition at the Levy Gallery served to proclaim the new stylistic turn of Dalí. According to the painter his surrealist period had come to a close and it was to be replaced by a return to Classicism and preoccupation with form. Despite the announcement of the artist, the works exhibited still dealt with irrational images, without posing a definitive break with the previous period.

After spending the summer at Del Monte Lodge, a unique resort located on the coast of California, in October 1941 Dalí moved to the city of New York in order to attend the premiere of *Labyrinth* at the Metropolitan Opera House, a ballet inspired by the myth of the minotaur and for which Dalí had prepared the libretto, sets and costumes. Starring the *Ballets Russes de Monte Carlo*, the show had a great impact and created the right atmosphere for the opening of a retrospective exhibition of Dalí and Miro organized by the Museum of Modern Art. The event, which was shown in eight more cities presented the artist as a genius gifted with a special talent for capturing the dark side of human existence.

The numerous glowing reviews in the press following the exhibition certified the love affair between the North American public and the painter, who totally eclipsed his fellow Catalan artist Joan Miró and managed to convey the idea that he was the true representative of Surrealism. Dalí's immense power of seduction was evident again in the autumn of the year 1942, when his autobiography became an instant bestseller.

NEXT PAGE, LEFT
**Dream Caused
by the Flight of a Bee
around a Pomegranate
a Second Before
Awakening**
1944
Oil on canvas
51 × 40.5 cm

PAGE 53, LEFT
**Dematerialization near
the Nose of Nero**
1947
Oil on canvas
76.5 × 46 cm

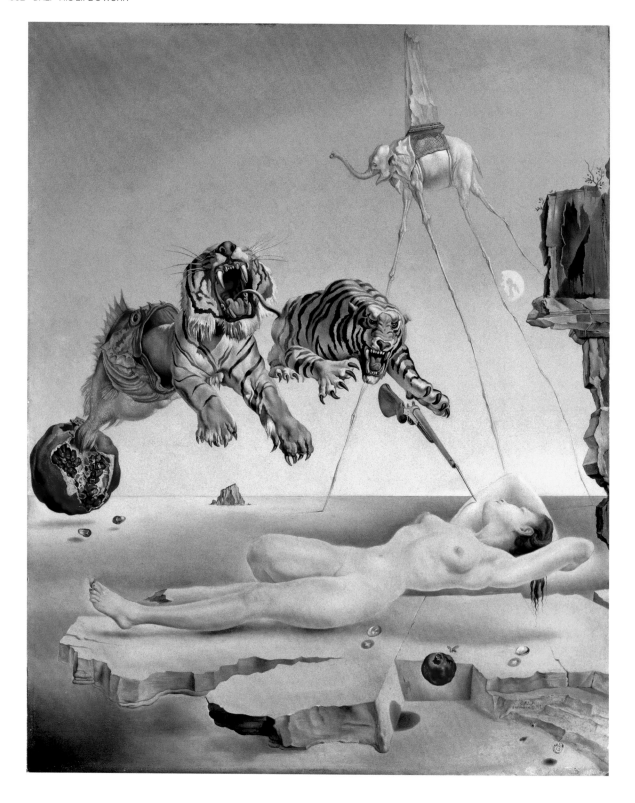

Financial stability

From 1943 Salvador Dalí obtained the financial backing of the married couple Reynolds and Eleanor Morse. The American collectors' interest in the Spanish painter's work allowed a regular income at what was a critical time for the art market, which was suffering the effects of World War II. The surrealist artist also carried out several society portraits and commissions for magazines, books and advertising campaigns. All these activities ensured economic stability, but left him less time available to focus on painting or more personal projects. Nonetheless, during his exile Dalí was able to produce works packed with symbolism, such as *Poetry of America*, which was ahead of the emergence of pop art with the inclusion of a bottle of Coca-Cola, and the suggestive *Dream Caused by the Flight of a Bee around a Pomegranate a Second Before Awakening*.

ABOVE RIGHT
Old Age, Adolescence and Infancy
1940. Oil on canvas
50.2 × 65 cm

BELOW RIGHT
Backdrop for the ballet Labyrinth
1941. Tempera on fabric
8.8 × 13 m

NEXT PAGE
The Apotheosis of Homer
Around 1945. Oil on canvas
63.7 × 116.7 cm

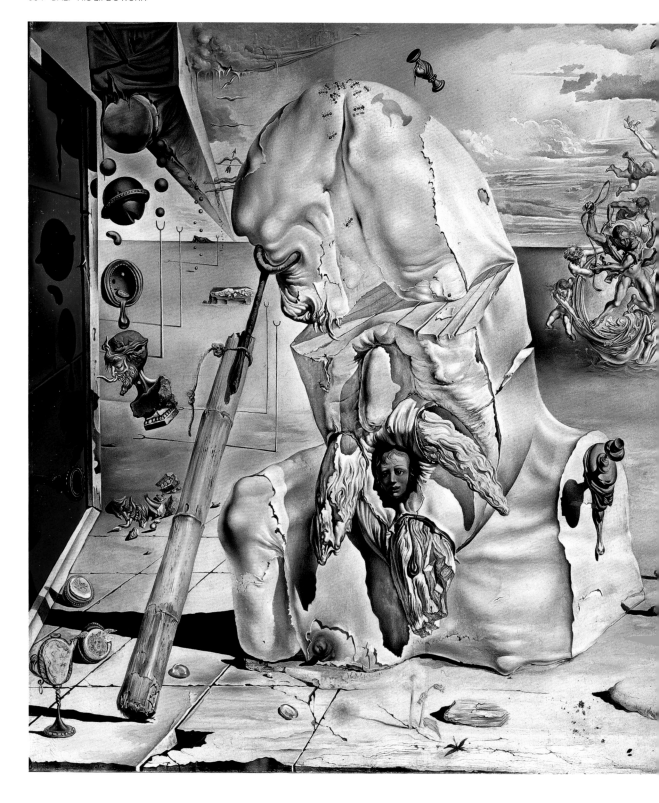

A multidisciplinary artist

Spurred by the success of his autobiography, in the autumn of 1943 Dalí began writing the novel *Rostros ocultos* (Hidden Faces), which was completed in just four months. Inspired by the narrative classics of Balzac and Stendhal, the book was a step further for the painter to be accepted as an all-round artist. This relentless pursuit of general recognition led Dalí to concatenate very varied experiences between 1944 and 1945: from the creation of *Mad Tristan* –considered as the first paranoiac ballet–, to a collaboration for the film *Spellbound*, of Alfred Hitchcock. Likewise, the artist exhibited his latest works in the *Bignou Gallery* of New York. Among the paintings on display included oneiric compositions such as *Uranium and Atomica Melancholica Idyll* (based on the bombing of Hiroshima, which triggered the interest of Dalí for nuclear physics) as well as very realistic oil paintings. One of these paintings of photographic quality was *Basket of*

PREVIOUS PAGE, LEFT
Basket of Bread
1945
Oil on canvas
33 × 38 cm

PREVIOUS PAGE, RIGHT
Geopoliticus Child Watching the Birth of the New Man
1943
Oil on canvas
45.4 × 50 cm

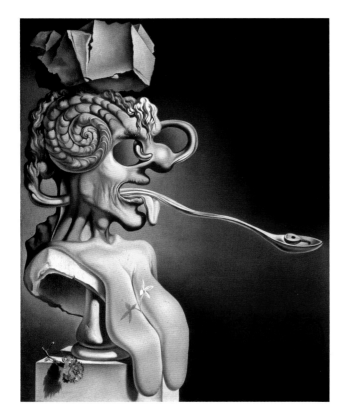

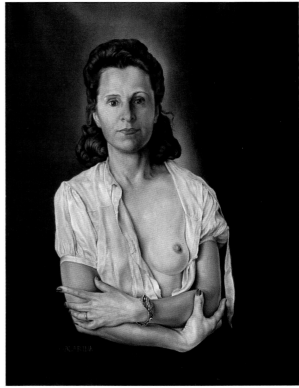

Bread, with which Dalí demonstrated his virtuosity to compose a still life scene heir of Velázquez, Zurbarán and Vermeer, masters of Baroque painting. The *Galarina* portrait, a tribute to Gala and Raphael's *La Fornarina* (*Portrait of a Young Woman*) to which the artist had devoted six months of work, was more proof of the technical expertise achieved by Dalí.

After the Bignou Gallery exhibition, Dalí kept up his strong productive output. In January 1946 he moved to California to work with the filmmaker Walt Disney on the production of a short film called *Destino (Destiny)*. Focused on the romance between a ballerina and a baseball player, the film's animation sought to use the major hallmarks of the painter, such as the landscape of Empordà and the use of double images. The lack of funds prevented the project from succeeding, and finally only one sequence of fifteen seconds got to be shot.

A new direction

The frustrating outcome of the collaboration with Disney did not alter the productive capacity of Dalí, who, in addition to illustrations for Shakespeare's *Macbeth* and *Don Quixote* by Miguel de Cervantes, again tried to become involved in the world of cinema by participating in a contest for the selection of a picture for the film *The Private Affairs of Bel Ami*. The painting produced by the artist for the competition was *The Temptation of Saint*

Anthony, a work which included one of his new icons, long-legged elephants carrying symbolic objects, and ideas that would gain prominence in subsequent years, such as mysticism and weightlessness.

In 1948 Dalí resumed his career as a writer with the publication of *50 Secrets of Magic Craftsmanship*. The book, packed with personal anecdotes, including all kinds of technical advice aimed at readers who aspired to follow in the footsteps of the artist. Through his unique sense of humour, Dalí insisted on the bringing back of Classicism and the legacy of artists such as Durer, Rembrandt, Ingres and Piero della Francesca. In addition to performing a furious attack on modern art, the text also included constant references to the absolute monarchy and expressed the desire of the painter to find faith. This reactionary discourse contributed to a reconciliation with the Spanish dictatorship, which ended up facilitating Dalí's return to his homeland. Thus, in July 1948, the artist put an end to his exile in the United States and sailed to Europe with Gala.

PREVIOUS PAGE, LEFT
Portrait of Pablo Picasso in the 21st century
1947. Oil on canvas
64.1 × 54.7 cm

PREVIOUS PAGE, RIGHT
Galarina
1944-1945
Oil on canvas
64.1 × 50.2 cm

BELOW
The Temptation of Saint Anthony
1946
Oil on canvas
89.7 × 119.5 cm

CHAPTER - 6

1949 - 1957
The Nuclear-Mystical period

When Dalí returned to Spain in the late forties it was an ultraconservative country where Surrealism had no place. The Franco regime, that considered that psychoanalysis was an immoral and unpatriotic practice, subordinated culture to its own propaganda interests, so that any form of expression liable to undermine the official ideology, which was based on the exaltation of the motherland and Catholicism, was persecuted. At this stage of intellectual suffocation, Dalí reinvented himself as an artist. The exploration of the unconscious gave way to harking back to the Italian Renaissance style and the study of Spanish mystics, such as the poet Saint John of the Cross. The painter fused his interest in Classicism and religion with the latest advances in atomic theory, a world which had obsessed the painter following the bombing of Hiroshima and Nagasaki. That combination of faith and science brought with it the creation of the nuclear-mystical style, of which Dalí was its sole representative.

A personal Catholicism

Dali opened his nuclear-mystical period with the painting *The Madonna of Portlligat*, a piece which he had already begun working on when in exile in the United States and two versions were made, the first one completed in Portlligat in the summer of 1949. Derived from the painting *Leda Atomica*, the oil painting showed the Virgin Mary with Gala's face floating in space, in a recreation of the Renaissance style of the subatomic universe. The unique Madonna conceived by Dalí obtained the approval of Pope Pius XII during a private hearing held in Rome in November of that year. After obtaining the admiration of the highest hierarch of the Catholic Church, the painter felt entitled to carry on working on that particular interpretation of Christian iconography and religious sentiment. In the following years, the creative path led to landmarks like *Christ of Saint John of the Cross*, a crucifixion scene in which the Catalan artist used his knowledge of baroque perspective and chiaroscuro.

The art of jewellery

Pure beauty

Dalí started in the world of jewellery in the United States with the assistance of Italian goldsmith Fulco di Verdura, who helped him make various brooches, watches, earrings and necklaces. Subsequently, the painter collaborated with the workshop of Carlos Alemany and Eric Ertman to develop a collection inspired by his own creative universe. The artist drew the pieces as accurately as possible, specifying the forms and colours that should be used. Dalí also indicated the ideal materials for each piece, based on the symbolic connotations of noble metals and precious stones. Based on these instructions, the artisans elaborated the pieces. According to Dalí, the resulting works were objects of pure beauty, designed to please the eye, elevate the soul and awaken the public's imagination.

❶ **The Royal Heart**
1953
Inside the heart-shaped piece of gold is an organic arrangement that is made up of rubies, diamonds, sapphires, emeralds and pearls that rhythmically move thanks to a motorised mechanism.

Dalí, 1971. The artist, in an exhibition of his jewellery, standing next to his work, the *Space Elephant*.

2 YEARS

silversmith Carlos Alemany took to create his five first jewels based on Dalí's designs.

❶

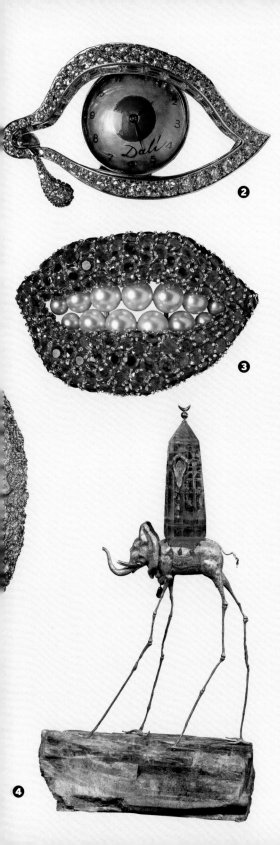

1958

IS THE YEAR

businessman Owen Cheatham's foundation acquired a large number of the jewels. The collection was exhibited in public on several occasions for charity.

②

The Eye of Time
1949
The eyelids are comprised of diamonds set in platinum surrounding a clock with a dial in three shades of blue enamel.

③

Ruby Lips
1949
Salvador Dalí employed yellow gold and individually set rubies for the lips, while he used thirteen pearls for the teeth.

1999

IS THE YEAR

in which the Theatre-Museum in Figueres bought Owen Cheatham's jewellery collection. The centre paid around five million euros for the pieces.

④

Space Elephant
1961
Used by Dalí in pictures such as *The Temptation of Saint Anthony*, the elephant is inspired by the obelisk of Rome's Plaza Minerva.

Tristan and Isolde. 1953. Gold, platinum and diamonds, it refers to Dalí's favourite opera.

Peace Medal. 1954. It combines yellow gold, diamonds and lapis lazuli.

Pax Vobiscum. 1968. The central piece opens to show a religious portrait.

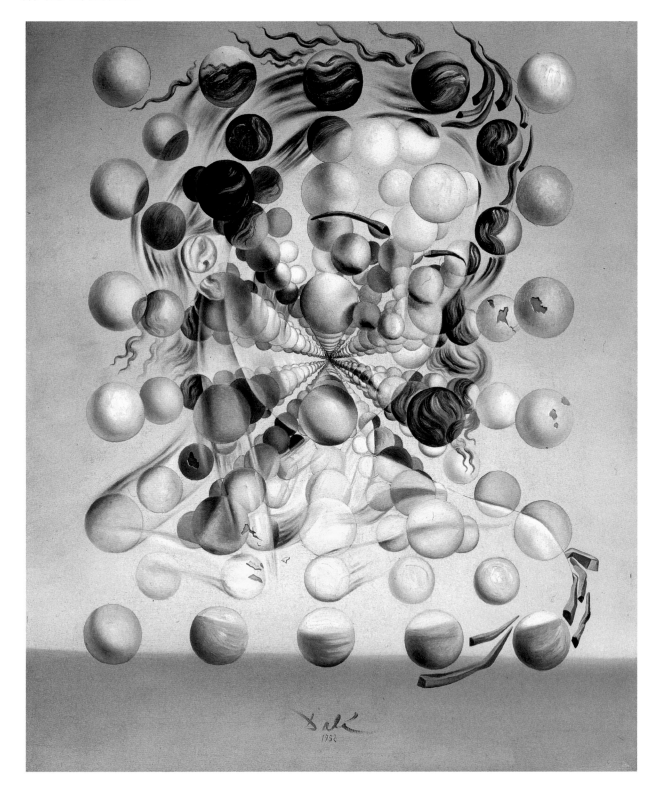

Mysticism and science

In the early fifties, Dalí tried to promote his new stylistic direction through several interviews, articles and conferences. One of the most symbolic appearances took place in October 1950 at the *Ateneo de Barcelona*, where two decades before the painter had shocked the audience with a vehement defense of Surrealism. On this occasion, the artist wanted to distance himself completely from the movement led by his former friend André Breton, as well as the plastic experiments of other avant-garde artists like Picasso, and inaugurated a splendid future for religious art, a style that, according to him, would allow Spain to regain its imperialist tradition.

The ideas of the Barcelona conference were reused in the *Mystical Manifesto*, a text published in April 1951 that proclaimed the decadence of contemporary art and the need for the so-called *Paranoiac-Critical Mysticism*, a painting genre based on the internalization of scientific advances and the pursuit of spiritual bliss. Dalí transferred this singular creative approach to works such as *The Ascension of Saint Cecilia* and *Galatea of the Spheres*, which generated images of three-dimensional appearance inspired by the theories of the splitting of the atom.

FORMER PAGE
Galatea of the Spheres
1952
Oil on canvas
65 × 54 cm

LEFT
The Ascension of Saint Cecilia
1955
Oil on canvas
81.5 × 66.5 cm

RIGHT
Young Virgin Auto-Sodomized by the Horns of Her Own Chastity
1954
Oil on canvas
40.5 × 30.5 cm

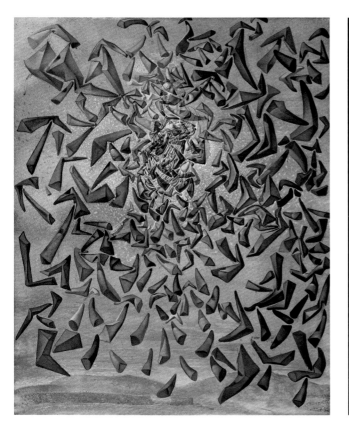

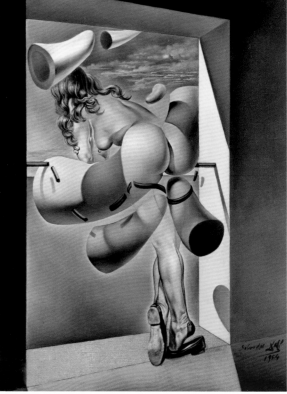

LEFT
**Raphaelesque Head
Exploding**
1951
Oil on canvas
43.2 × 33.1 cm

RIGHT
**Assumpta Corpuscularia
Lapislazulina**
1952
Oil on canvas
230 × 144 cm

The myth of the rhinocerous

Dalí's research on the organisation of matter led to the emergence of an recurring image: the rhino horn. According to the artist, this image, which he claimed to have seen in the painting *The Lacemaker* by Vermeer was the perfect representation of the logarithmic form around which all elements are structured. Interpreted by Dalí as a symbol of extreme irrationality, the rhinoceros also fitted in with *The Songs of Maldoror*, an experimental text written in the nineteenth century by the Count of Lautréamont –the pseudonym of Uruguayan writer Isidore Ducasse– in which God is metamorphosed into that animal. The work, considered a forerunner of Surrealism, was well-known by Dalí, who had even managed to carry out a series of illustrations in the 1930's for a special edition of the book. Rhinocerous horns started to work their way into various works carried out at the start of the decade of the fifties, amongst them *Raphaelesque Head Exploding* and *Assumpta Corpuscularia Lapislazulina*, and their use intensified up to 1954. During that year, the artist explained the importance of his new favourite icon in com-

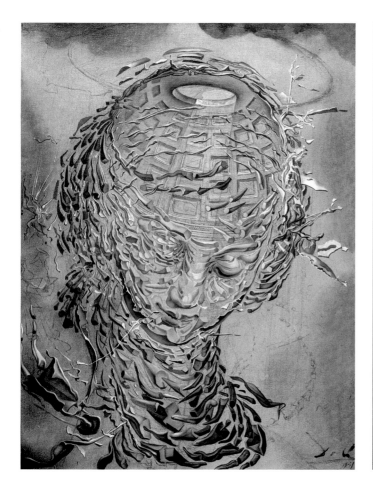

ABOVE
**Rhinocerontic Figures
of Illisus of Phidias**
1954
Oil on canvas
101.5 × 131 cm

positions such as *Young Virgin Auto-Sodomized by the Horns of her Own Chastity*, based on an photograph from *Playboy* magazine, and *Rhinocerontic Figures of Illisus of Phidias*, where one of the sculptures that decorate the Parthenon of the Acropolis of Athens breaks down into dozens of horns. Dalí alternated his fascination with rhinocerous horns with the field of biochemistry. After the scientists James Watson and Francis Crick published the description of the DNA structure in the year 1953, the painter became absolutely fascinated and captivated by the scientific world of molecules. According to the Catalan artist, DNA, the base of life, was the real proof of the existence of God. By means of this interpretation, molecular language fitted perfectly in with the Mystical Paranoiac-Critical vision, enriching the imagination of a painter who always kept abreast of the latest scientific advances happening in the world.

CHAPTER - 7

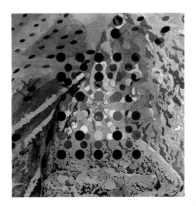

1958 - 1989
The final obsessions

In the final stretch of his career, Salvador Dalí saw his efforts recognised. Now transformed into an international celebrity thanks to his constant presence in the media, the Catalan artist became the subject of numerous retrospectives at major museums. The exhibitions unveiled the artist's work to new generations around the world, while confirming the validity of a legacy that Dalí never stopped expanding. In fact, in his last years the painter showed himself to be a multifaceted character, combining deep respect for tradition with experiments that pushed the boundaries of art. Through the tributes to old masters, Dalí completely distanced himself from most of his contemporaries, showing his strong personality and meticulous technique, while with the adoption of new technologies such as holography, the painter formally renewed his work and deepened his concern for the visual relationship established between the canvas and the viewer.

Solemn scenes

In the late fifties Salvador Dalí began work on a series of works of monumental dimensions focused on religious and historical topics. With those pictures, distinguished by using large panoramic and obsessive attention-to-detail, the Catalan artist wanted to pay tribute to the French academic painting of the nineteenth century, a tradition reviled by fans of modern art because of its flamboyant character.

The Discovery of America by Christopher Columbus was one of the first works developed by Dalí under these new creative parameters. Commissioned by American magnate Huntington Hartford for the gallery of modern art he was planning in Columbus Circle Square in New York, the oil –originally titled *The Dream of Columbus*– shows an adolescent Christopher Columbus carrying a banner with a virginal representation of Gala, an allegory of the arrival of Catholicism to the Americas. On the other hand, in the right half of the painting dozens of spears appear in tribute to *The Surrender of Breda*, the famous painting by Velázquez, while the lower end is dominated by a sea urchin, a symbol previously used by the painter to refer to his childhood in Cadaqués.

Dalí's stylistic twist was met with hostility by most of the critics, who preferred the abstract compositions of the prevailing avant-garde movements to the Classicism of the Catalan artist. However, the painter stayed true to his artistic vision and in the sixties continued to develop similar works, such as *The Ecumenical Council*, inspired by the Second Vatican Council, convened by Pope John XXIII in 1959.

The renewal of the past

A large sum of elements

During his mature artistic period Dalí seized many of the technical and iconographic resources that he had developed in earlier periods. Thus, the use of double images (one of the main contributions of the paranoiac-critical method, developed by the painter in the thirties) could maintain its validity thanks to its presence in later works like *The Hallucinogenic Toreador*. Considered one of the artist's most complex works, the work combines diverse representations of the Venus de Milo with flies, atomic particles and the rocky landscape of Cape Creus to generate the figure of a bullfighter.

New York, 1973
Salvador Dalí, with the musician Alice Cooper, with whom he formed a brief artistic collaboration.

The Hallucinogenic Toreador
1968-1970
Oil on canvas
398.8 × 299.7 cm

16
MONTHS
of work were needed by Dalí to complete *The Hallucinogenic Toreador*. The work was object of several previous studies that served to define the double images employed.

Childhood memory
The child dressed as a sailor that holds a hoop and a femur is a representation of Dalí. The painter already used this figure in *The Spectre of Sex-Appeal*, of 1934.

1947
IS THE YEAR
bullfighter Manolete died, who might be the figure that appears in Dalí's painting. It is also believed that the painter was inspired by a poem by Lorca in tribute to the bullfighter Sánchez Mejías.

1970

IS THE YEAR
American patron
Reynolds Morse
bought *The Hallu-
cinogenic Toreador*.

Personal work
The image of the bull-
fighter symbolises
the friends of Dalí
that died young.

**Study for
The Hallucinogenic
Toreador**
1968. Oil on canvas
57.4 × 44.5 cm

***Athens is Burning!* –
The School of
Athens and the Fire
in the Borgo**
1979-1980
Oil on wood
32.2 × 43.1 cm

Venus de Milo
According to Dalí, the
bullfighter figure
came to him when
contemplating the
sculptured figure on
a pencil box label.

Formal innovations

Parting from *Hallucinogenic Toreador*,
between 1968 and 1970 Dalí did various
paintings of a square metre centered on
fragments of the original composition.
The artist's interest in deepening the
perception of pictorial space was a fore-
taste of later optical experiments such as
Athens is Burning!, a work in which
Dalí turned to stereoscopy to superim-
pose two paintings by Raphael, *The
School of Athens* and *the Fire in the Borgo*.

The omnipresence of Gala

On the 8th of August, 1958 Dalí and Gala got married by the Church in an small private ceremony in the sanctuary of the church Mare de Déu dels Àngels, located a few kilometres from the city of Girona, in northern Catalonia. With this commitment, the painter demonstrated the affection he still felt for whom was his wife, muse, artistic representative and administrator. Always idealised, the representation of the figure of Gala took up a large part of Dalí's production in the sixties and seventies. *Gala, Nude from Behind* was one of the most emblematic works of that period. With precise strokes and a luminous palette, Dalí highlighted the sensuality of his wife with a classical composition inspired by the painting *The Valpinçon Bather*, which had been carried out in 1806 by Ingres. Gala's back as a reflection of the ideal of feminine beauty also protagonised *Gala Nude Looking at the Sea which at 18 metres appears the President Lincoln*. Converted into a renewal of the work carried out in his younger period *Figure at a Window*, the composition pointed to the future incorporating concepts typical of cybernetics, which allowed to create an optical illusion starting from a digital interpretation of the face of American President Abraham Lincoln, obtained by investigator Leon D. Harmon.

Perpignan and the centre of the world

Salvador Dalí's catalogue of obsessions increased in the mid-sixties with the railway station of the French city of Perpignan, a place which the artist went to in order to travel to Paris. According to the painter, the station acted as a frontier between his private life and public activity. Going through Perpignan meant leaving behind months of isolation and tranquility in Portlligat in order to head for frenetic Parisian life. Also, the Catalan artist claimed that whenever he approached the station he could think of all kinds of great ideas, to the point that he was able to enter in a state of ecstasy. Dalí's fixation with the place was reflected in *The Railway Station at Perpignan*, a composition in which the artist synthesized his creative world. In the centre of the canvas, where Jesus Christ appears on the cross and a figure levitating, the painter made four beams of light converge to stage the centrality of Perpignan, while the two far ends of the composition placed several references to *The Angelus* of Millet.

ABOVE
The Railway Station at Perpignan
1965
Oil on canvas
295 × 406 cm

Apotheosis of the Dollar. 1965. Oil on canvas. 300 × 400 cm

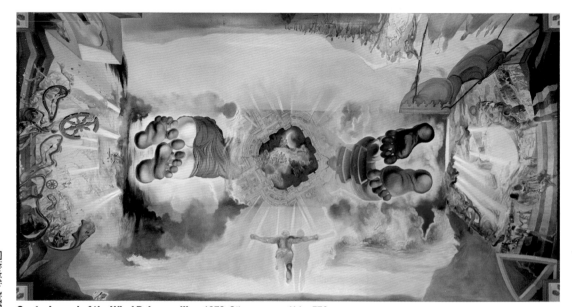

Central panel of the Wind Palace ceiling. 1972. Oil on canvas. 114 × 570 cm

The legacy of a genius

From the 1970's Dalí reduced his painting activity, but not his desire to surprise the public. Inspired by the work of baroque portrait painter Gerard Dou, the artist began studying stereoscopy, a technique that allowed the creation of a relief effect from the use of two almost identical pictures and a mirror system. The painter alternated this method, which resulted in compositions such as *Dalí Seen from the Back Painting Gala from the Back Eternalized by Six Virtual Corneas Provisionally Reflected by Six Real Mirrors*, with holography, a recent invention that used lasers to generate three-dimensional images. According to Dalí, using the third dimension aspired not only to convey to the viewer the impression of depth, but access to immortality.

In parallel to his optical experiments, the painter promoted the creation of the Dalí Theatre-Museum in Figueres, which opened its doors in 1974. The centre was located in a former run down municipal theatre that in 1919 had hosted the Catalan artist's first exhibition. With the intention of creating a gigantic surrealist object, Dalí directly oversaw the construction process, taking part in the design of all details and creating works intended specifically for the space, like the painting that decorates the vault of the Palacio del Viento (Wind Palace). The result was the definitive compendium of the path of a character with a vivid imagination, possessor of one of the most original creative universes of art history.

LEFT
Dalí's Hand Drawing Back the Golden Fleece in the Form of a Cloud to Show Gala the Dawn, Completely Nude, Very, Very Far Away Behind the Sun
1977
Oil on canvas, stereoscopic work on two panels
60 × 60 cm

RIGHT
Dalí Seen from the Back Painting Gala from the Back Eternalized by Six Virtual Corneas Provisionally Reflected by Six Real Mirrors
1972-1973
Oil on canvas
60.5 × 60.5 cm

SALVADOR DALÍ. HIS LIFE'S WORK
CONCEPT AND MANAGEMENT OF PROJECT: CARLOS GIORDANO AND NICOLÁS PALMISANO
COORDINATION: MARTA DE LA SERNA
CONTENTS: DANIEL R. CARUNCHO
LAYOUT: TONI BERNARDINO
PHOTOGRAPHIC RETOUCHING: JAVIER ORDUÑA

PUBLISHED BY
© DOS DE ARTE EDICIONES, S.L., BARCELONA, 2020

TEXTS
MANAGEMENT AND COORDINATION: DOS DE ARTE EDICIONES, S.L.
WRITER: DANIEL R. CARUNCHO
TRANSLATION: CERYS GIORDANO JONES
© DOS DE ARTE EDICIONES, S.L., BARCELONA, 2020

SALVADOR DALÍ
OF THE WORKS OF SALVADOR DALÍ:
© SALVADOR DALÍ, FUNDACIÓ GALA-SALVADOR DALÍ, VEGAP, FIGUERES, 2020
 • PAGES 17 (ABOVE LEFT), 26 (BELOW LEFT), 31 (ABOVE LEFT, BELOW LEFT), 32, 34 (ABOVE RIGHT), 51,
53 (ABOVE RIGHT), 56 (ABOVE RIGHT) AND FLAP, 72 (RIGHT), 71 AND 74-75 (CENTRE) AND FLAP, 73.
© SALVADOR DALÍ, FUNDACIÓ GALA-SALVADOR DALÍ, VEGAP, 2020
COLLECTION OF THE SALVADOR DALÍ MUSEUM, ST PETERSBURG, FLORIDA
 • PAGE 62 (RIGHT). © CSG CIC GLASGOW MUSEUMS AND LIBRARIES COLLECTIONS

THE RIGHTS OF IMAGE OF SALVADOR DALÍ RESERVED. FUNDACIÓ GALA-SALVADOR DALÍ, FIGUERES, 2020

PHOTOGRAPHS/IMAGES
• FLAP. ALBUM/AKG/DIEUZAIDE
• BACK COVER (SALVADOR DALÍ) AND INSIDE COVER. ALBUM/RDA/ROBERT COHEN
• INSIDE COVER. ALBUM/RUE DES ARCHIVES / BRIDGEMAN IMAGES / AGIP
• PAGES 2 (ABOVE), 60 © DANIEL FARSON/GETTY IMAGES
• PAGES 2 (BELOW), 3 (EXCEPT DALÍ PORTRAIT), 5, 7, 8 (ABOVE), 9 (CENTRE), 12, 13, 14, 15, 16, 17, 18, 19, 21, 23, 24, 25, 26
(BELOW LEFT, BELOW RIGHT), 27, 28 (LEFT), 29 (SURREALIST OBJECT), 30, 31, 32, 33, 34, 36, 37 (LEFT), 39, 42, 43
(BELOW), 46 (ABOVE LEFT AND RIGHT), 49, 50, 51, 52, 53, 56, 57, 58, 61, 63, 64 (CENTRE), 65, 66, 67, 69, 71, 72, 73, 74-75
(CENTRE), 74 (CENTRE AND BELOW LEFT), 75 (ABOVE RIGHT AND CENTRE LEFT), 76, 78, 79. COVER, BACK COVER
AND REAR FLAP © FUNDACIÓ GALA-SALVADOR DALÍ, FIGUERES, 2020
• PAGES 3. (BELOW) AND 48. SELZNICK/UNITED ARTISTS/ALBUM
• PAGE 4. ULLSTEIN BILD/GETTY IMAGES
• PAGES 6-7. REPORTES ASSOCIES/ GETTY IMAGES
• PAGE 6 (LEFT). ALBUM/MONDADORI PORTFOLIO
• PAGE 8 (BELOW). MANUEL LITRAN/GETTY IMAGES
• PAGE 8 (RIGHT). ALBUM
• PAGE 9 (ABOVE RIGHT). IBERFOTO/PHOTOAISA
• PAGE 9 (BELOW RIGHT). © AFP/GETTY IMAGES
• PAGES 10-11, 29 (RIGHT CENTRE AND BELOW RIGHT). AUTHORS: CARLOS GIORDANO AND NICOLÁS PALMISANO ©
DOS DE ARTE EDICIONES S.L., BARCELONA, 2020
• PAGE 20. AUTHOR: LUIS BUÑUEL © FUNDACIÓ GALA-SALVADOR DALÍ, FIGUERES, 2020
• PAGES 22 , 44-45 (CENTRE). ALBUM/CULTURE-IMAGES
• PAGES 26 (ABOVE), 29 (LOBSTER-TELEPHONE, VENUS DE MILO WITH DRAWERS) 43 (ABOVE), 46(BELOW),
68 (LEFT). ALBUM/AKG-IMAGES
• PAGES 28-29 (RETROSPECTIVE BUST OF WOMAN). © DE AGOSTINI/G. DAGLI ORTI/AGE FOTOSTOCK
• PAGE 29 (ABOVE RIGHT). ROLLS PRESS/POPPERFOTO/GETTY IMAGES
• PAGE 29 (THE MAE WEST LIPS SOFA). ALBUM/DPA
• PAGE 35. MODERNA MUSEET, STOCKHOLM, SWEDEN © DE AGOSTINI PICTURE LIBRARY/D. DAGLI ORIT/
BRIDGEMAN IMAGES
• PAGE 37 (RIGHT). PHOTOGRAPHY © THE ART INSTITUTE OF CHICAGO
• PAGE 38 © BETTMANN/ GETTY IMAGES
• PAGE 40 (LEFT). © BRIDGEMAN IMAGES/AGE FOTOSTOCK
• PAGE 40 (RIGHT), 47. MUSEUM BOYMANS VANBEUNINGEN, ROTTERDAM, NETHERLANDS/BRIDGEMAN IMAGES
• PAGE 41, 45 (BELOW RIGHT). ALBUM/JOSEPH MARTIN
• PAGE 44 (BELOW LEFT). PHOTO © AGIP/BRIDGEMAN IMAGES
• PAGE 45 (ABOVE RIGHT). © ART MEDIA/AGE FOTOSTOCK
• PAGES 54-55 © BPK/BAYERISCHE STAATSGEMÄLDESAMMLUNGEN-SAMMLUNG MODERNE KUNST IN DER
PINAKOTHEK DER MODERNE MÜNCHEN
• PAGE 59. AUTHOR : J. GELEYNS/RO SCAN/© [ROYAL MUSEUMS OF FINE ARTS OF BELGIUM, BRUSSELS]
• PAGE 62 (LEFT). MARQUETTE UNIVERSITY FINE ART COMMITTEE, MILWAUKEE, WI, USA/BRIDGEMAN IMAGES
• PAGE 62 (RIGHT). © CSG CIC GLASGOW MUSEUMS AND LIBRARIES COLLECTIONS
• PAGE 64 (BELOW LEFT). © INA/ GETTY IMAGES
• PAGE 68 (RIGHT). PRIVATE COLLECTION PHOTO © CHRISTIE'S IMAGES/BRIDGEMAN IMAGES
• PAGE 70. KAMMERMAN/GETTY IMAGES
• PAGE 75 (VENUS DE MILO). ALBUM/ORONOZ
• PAGE 77. (PHOTO: ©) RHEINISCHES BILDARCHIV KÖLN, RBA_D033360

dosde

www.dosde.com

EDITION 2020

SKU: 45-002-01 / 06
ISBN: 978-84-9103-033-1
LEGAL DEPOSIT: B 1964-2020
PRINTED IN SPAIN

WWW.DOSDE.COM